Wrongful DEATH

Wrongful
DEATH

HEATHER T EDGELL

Wrongful Death

Copyright © 2023 by Heather T. Edgell

All rights reserved

No portion of this book may be reproduced, stored in
a retrieval system, or transmitted in any form by any
means—electronic, mechanical, photocopy, recording,
or other—except for brief quotations in printed reviews,
without prior permission of the author.

First Edition

Hardcover ISBN: 979-8-8229-1668-5
Paperback ISBN: 979-8-8229-1669-2
eBook ISBN: 979-8-8229-1670-8

On a beautiful sunshining Tuesday, August 25, 1942, my mom, Janice F. Powell, was born. She was the beautiful daughter to Joseph and Olga Powell who was their eleventh and final child to be born. Joseph and Olga owned a farm and a small store where Mom spent most of her time, other than school in the summer, helping. Mom came from a very loving and Christian home with a very loving family. She was always in church, from when she was a young girl well into adulthood.

Mom had such an amazing voice, and she loved to sing. She sounded just like Loretta Lynn, and she was in many different talent shows.

Mom

My mom's parents were very humble and kind. Her mom, Olga, passed away in 1987 from congestive heart failure at the tender age of eighty-seven. Her dad, Joseph, passed away in 1989 from old age at the age of eighty-nine. They were married for sixty-nine glorious years and watched seven of their children be buried.

Mom married my dad, Wilbur Grizzard (aka Bud) on June 6, 1959. After getting married, they got involved with running different types of businesses. To name a few they had: Bud's Glass Company, Western Drive-In (a restaurant), and Country Girl Drive-In (a restaurant and lounge). As life went on by, they had four children: Wanda, born July 11, 1960; Heather (me), born June 23, 1961; Johnny, born February 29, 1964; and Renee, born November 16, 1965. Mom loved all her kids with every bit in her as much as she loved her life. Mom was so very humble and kind; she would give the shirt off her back to anyone who was in need. One of her greatest accomplishments was being the top sales lady with the Olan Mills picture studio, with seventy sales in twenty-four hours.

Mom's accomplishments at work

Having four kids and running their three businesses kept Mom very active. However, in 1971, due to my father's alcoholism and abuse, they divorced. But that never stopped my mom from wearing a smile on her face and keeping positive, bright-eyed, and considerate to everyone around her despite all she had gone through.

In 1972, my mom would remarry a man, GE Chambers, who ultimately lost his life due to brain cancer. This happened right around the time that I was finishing school. My dad (Bud) had disappeared off to Mexico so that he would not have to pay my mom any child support, and he wanted to carry on with his life. As graceful as Mom was, she continued to run all her businesses and still maintained being a mother and taking care of her children.

Mom on bowling league

For years Mom was in three bowling leagues until January 2016 while running different businesses. She also had a florist shop and an arcade among many other businesses. She was one to be known as the business lady and carried herself well as she always did. She did not like confrontation at all and avoided it at all costs.

Mom bowling league

We all finished school and went our separate ways into adulthood, choosing different careers and such, but we were always so delighted to visit and spend time with our mom. We took vacations together, from going to the mountains and sitting by the stream talking about everything to having cookouts at the cabin, and we always enjoyed watching the Indians dance.

Vacation in the mountains

Johnny spent most of his adult life living in Fredericksburg, Virginia, and then moved to Tampa, Florida, where he still resides. I, Heather, spent most of my life in Jacksonville, North Carolina, with a brief stint in Charlotte, North Carolina, but am now residing back in Jacksonville. Wanda lived in Jacksonville, North Carolina, for a few years, then moved to Atlanta, Georgia, with her eldest daughter, then moved to Temple, Texas, where she still lives. In 1985, Renee and her husband Rick were stationed in Jacksonville, North Carolina, where Mom went to live with

Vacation

them. Being in the military, they were stationed in Quantico, Virginia. Rick and Renee came back to Jacksonville, North Carolina, and Mom stayed with them until February 15, 2015. Throughout these years, all her children gave her seven grandchildren, who all loved her dearly.

Mom, 73 years old

I returned from Charlotte, and Mom moved in with me. We would always go on vacations, go out to eat, go shopping—just anything that involved enjoying life. One thing Mom loved to do was play bingo. At this time, Mom was healthy; she was never really on any medication, except for a low-dose blood pressure medicine. It was only ten milligrams and did not affect her everyday life, and she was not on any other medication. When Mom was in pain, such as a headache, she would only take Tylenol. Other than that, she was completely healthy.

Then on February 8, 2016, our whole world changed. Mom fell at my house, and I called 911. EMS came and brought her to the hospital. She stayed there for ten days, but there was no bleeding. Her heart rate had just dropped dramatically all the way down to thirty-eight. She did have some swelling, but that was it. The whole time she was admitted, she would just lie in the bed, so that led them to put her into a rehabilitation center at a local nursing home. During Mom's stay there, the nursing staff dropped her on several occasions. There was one instance where Mom told me that someone hit her from behind while she was in a wheelchair.

Nobody at this nursing home stated to me or my sister, who had power of attorney at this time, what had taken place. We unfortunately had to go to the hospital on many occasions because of all the falls that took place in rehab. Because of this, they made her a permanent resident.

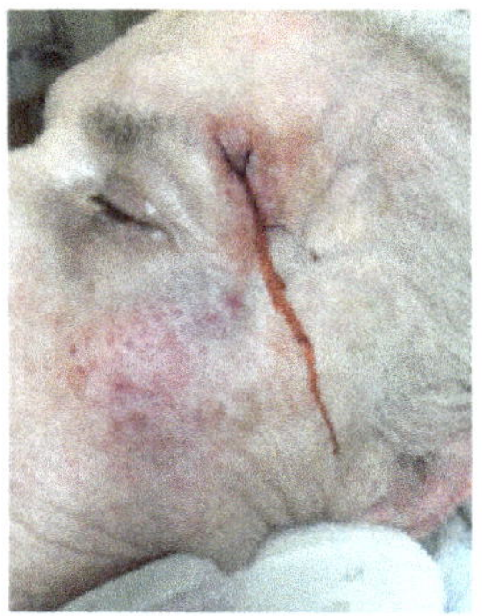

Mom was hit from behind by employee
and state said no findings

Not long after they made Mom a resident of the nursing home, a certified nursing assistant (CNA) pulled me to the side to let me know that one of the nurses had scratched Mom's back completely up. I then called my sister to come help me with this, which eventually ended up with me calling 911 to make a report, but of course the police stated that they could find no findings that it was, in fact, an employee at the facility. My sister and I were then "red-flagged" by the nursing home, which meant that we could not get our mom transferred to another facility, which was a complete and total nightmare.

We also decided to call the state of North Carolina for elderly abuse, but again, no findings.

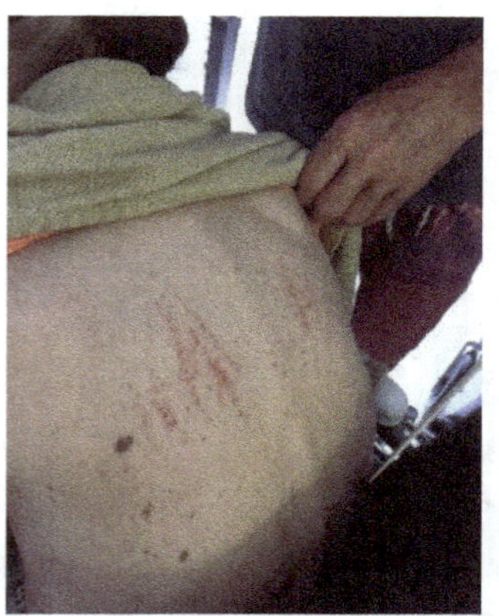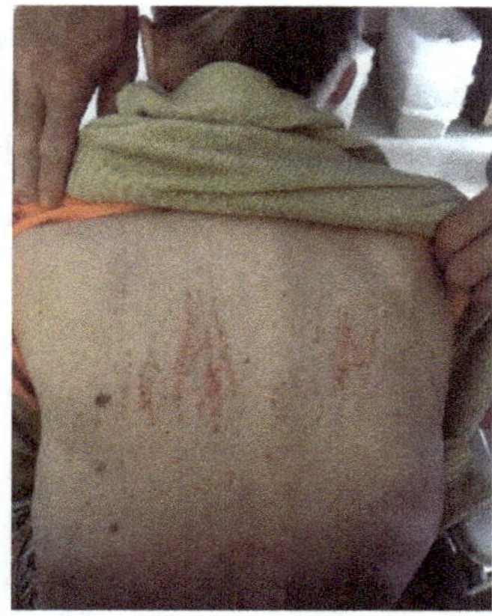

Mom's back clawed up by nurse; no findings

Since Mom was now a resident, we wanted to make sure we visited her as often as possible, especially with all the incidents that were happening. We would go see Mom every day for lunch between one and two p.m. for their daily lunchtime plates. We walked in on one occasion, and the plate was so far away from her that she couldn't even reach the food or drink if she was hungry or thirsty. There were also several times that the food was cold. I walked in on her crying one day, sitting in her wheelchair, with her face almost in her food. She was left with no one to feed her or help her. Almost every visit, we would come in and her diaper was filled with urine and feces, which let to us always going to find a staff member to come and change her, because we were not allowed to change her; it had to be a CNA, and when they would do it, we would always have to wait in the hallway. We were never allowed to be in the room when they changed our mother.

Floors wet all the time

Bathroom floor wet

There was one day when I was out back and was about to leave to head home, and I decided that I would just go back in and check on her one last time before leaving. She was not in her room. Since there was a big shower room down the hall from her room, I decided to open the door, and she was sitting in a wheelchair, slumped over, with nobody in there with her. All alone. I found the CNA and asked her why my mom was alone, with her response being, "I have something else to do." No patients were allowed to be alone during shower time; however, my mom was left alone. Because of this, I decided to wait with my mom until the CNA came back in and helped mom get her shower. At this point, the CNA advised me that they were severely understaffed.

On another visit, Mom was dropped once again, but this time it caused bleeding on the left side of her head. This started the numerous hospital visits. Several trips were because Mom was dehydrated because they would not give her anything to drink. We would have to be there to ensure that she was being fed and given something to drink. With all of these accidents, not once did the nursing home decide to call me or my sister, who had POA. Neither one of us knew anything unless we went there or called. Visualize that! There were so many days when my sister and I would take turns to ensure that someone was always there with Mom. Some days I would go in at two p.m. just to see if they had fed her, and as always the table was pushed so far away from her that she could not eat or drink even if she wanted to.

We went out and bought Mom some new clothes, pajamas and such, all name brands. However, for some reason her clothes started to come up missing. I always did Mom's laundry every week, and my sister bought 90 percent of the clothes with her name on the tag. We never understood where the clothes were going.

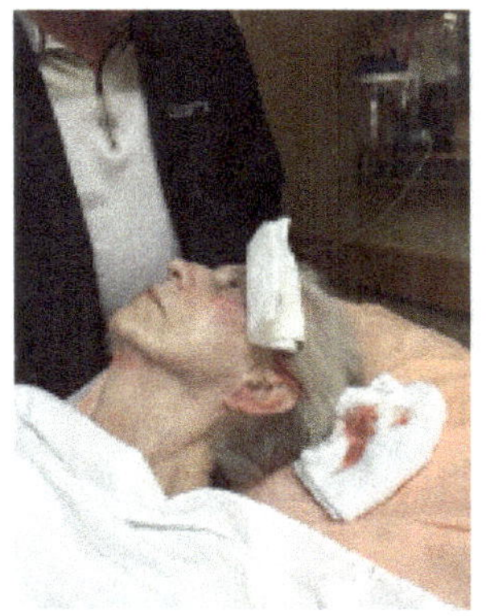

Mom's visit to hospital
to get stitches

With work, family, and the lives that we were living, we tried to put our trust into the nursing home to get complete and honest updates, which was something that we never got. Everything was always a cover-up story when it came to my mom, along with other patients who we witnessed, but I will not mention those patients' names. The abuse that the nursing home brought to their patients was overwhelming. The lack of care was so horrible, and if they had not red-flagged us, we would have been able to move our mom to another facility.

Again, we called the state and 911 several times, but there were always "no findings," and there was not much else we could do. Where would the other one hundred patients be taken to had they found them in the wrong? The CNAs there stated that they had twenty to thirty patients each shift, so how could they help all these people? This was why everyone was always so neglected. This was the main reason why we wanted to be there as much as we could. I would always question the staff about the treatment, and every day and every time they would yell, "*We are understaffed!*" We heard this every day the entire time that our mom was there. There were even multiple occasions where my sister Renee and I would help other patients if we were able to. The nursing home did not even care that we were unlicensed individuals helping other patients. Often times, I would look down the hall and see the staff on their cell phones hiding out back and in the smoking area. It was horrible all the time, and again we called state and there were "*No findings!*"

On my birthday in 2018, I decided to go in and have breakfast with Mom. I stayed until ten a.m., as I was heading to the beach to celebrate my birthday. When I returned from the beach at two p.m., Mom was lying on her back with her head to the left. She seemed more distant than when I'd left her earlier that morning. Something was not right, but my sister and I had never received a call about what happened while we were gone. Suddenly, she was struggling to talk and even swallow. At eight p.m. the same night, a male CNA came in to help me pull my mom up in the bed, and Mom kept mumbling over and over, "It wasn't my fault." I asked the CNA what she meant by "It was not her fault," to which he stated he did not know. As you can see, the state findings state that her doctor was not even notified of her being hung from the hover lift. That was what happened to Mom; there was only one person assisting in getting her out of the bed, and Mom fell from the lift. Once that happened, she was unable to swallow or talk.

Then on July 7, 2018, I went into the room and there was an awful smell. Mom pointed to her lower back, obviously in pain, so I went to the nurse's station to tell her my mom had stated her back hurt. They gave me a tube of Bengay. I closed Mom's door and went to take her Depends down. The pain was not something muscular; it was a huge bedsore, one so big that you could put your fist inside of it. It had to have been on there for several months; however, nobody had ever told us about this, and no one had bothered to even document it. We reported this to state there was nothing in her records, only being hung by the lift. This bedsore was what ultimately killed her.

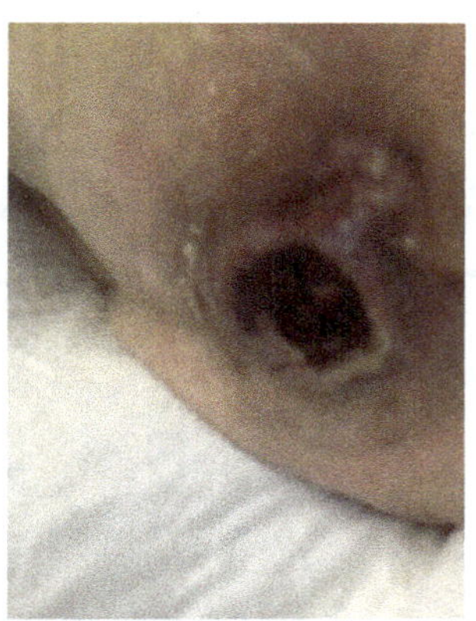

Bed sore we were never told about until I Heather found it July 7, 2018. E.coli had already taken over her body.

We even have some video clippings of the CNA changing Mom alone in the room. She was playing on her phone before even changing her and continued after. All the while, Mom's head was left on the metal bar on the bed. Again, we made a report to the state. This time, they came in to inspect the facility. This was August 2, 2018, and the very next day was when we received the news that Mom had been hanging from the lift on June 23, even though it had nothing to do with the bedsore or the recent complaints that we'd made against the nursing home.

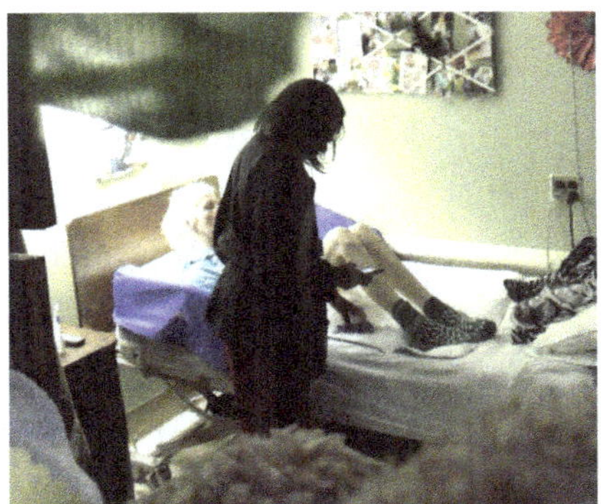

CAN playing on her phone when she was supposed to be changing mom

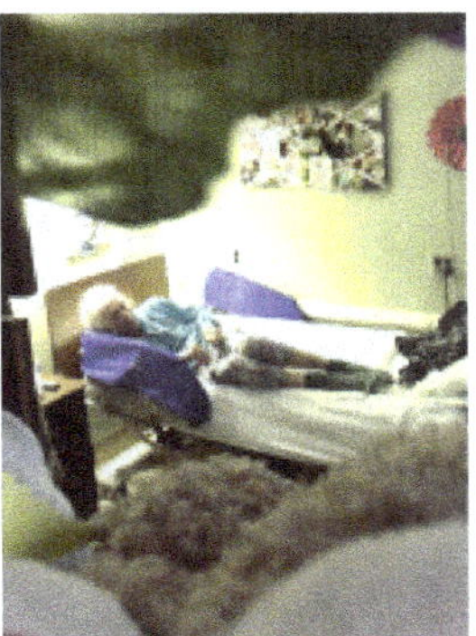

CNA playing on her cell while mom had to lay on the metal bar

From July 7, 2018 to August 3, 2018 (which was when my mom passed away at 6:30 a.m. EST), hospice would come in and feed Mom since the nursing home was not. During that time frame, Mom gained about ten pounds because they were taking care of her. We still were never informed of anything about the bedsore except that if proper wound care had been administered, we could've gotten it debrided, and she would have been able to sustain life. We were always left with no information, no updates, nothing. During this time, my sister and I were informed by the nurse that unfortunately it was too late and E. coli from the bedsore had set in and had taken over her body. There was nothing that we could do.

We could never understand why we were never told anything. My sister had POA. Someone was always there with her. Why not tell us? We feel 100 percent that this was an extreme cover-up by the nursing home. We contacted the state even after her passing because we wanted all their findings. When those came back, they only mentioned the hanging, never the bedsore. I slept on the floor for three days and three nights as she was passing. Nobody ever investigated her death; they didn't investigate anything!

This has affected me and my siblings in a lot of ways. We have a lot of health problems due to the overwhelming stress and the things we watched Mom endure at the nursing home. Wanda ended up with post-traumatic stress disorder (PTSD), high blood pressure, and major depression. I ended up with PTSD, high blood pressure, and major depression. Johnny ended up with PTSD, high blood pressure, and major depression, and he suffered a stroke. Renee ended up with PTSD and major depression.

Mom never complained about anything; she was always smiling. She did not have to die the way she did. All of what happened could have been prevented. But nobody would listen to us: not the nursing home, not even the state of North Carolina. We had no outlet that would even listen to us.

Mom's gravesite

We miss our mom. We just want the truth, and that's the main reason behind writing this short book. I want everyone to be aware of what really goes on in these facilities. We are still grieving. Had Mom died of natural causes, we would have been able to handle it differently and grieved appropriately. But with the abuse and neglect that we witnessed firsthand, we are not able to move on, and we are attending counseling over this.

You can see all of the findings from the state. We retained a lawyer, but he advised us that it would be so hard to fight the state because with the limited nursing homes, there is nowhere else for the other patients to go. We now call the nursing home "the slaughterhouse."

When Mom was admitted to this nursing home from the hospital, they told us that she had Alzheimer's or dementia; however, none of the paperwork from the nursing home or state show that this was the reason she was admitted. We will forever be left in the dark with no closure.

Mom loved her children, family, and friends so much. She was the most beautiful lady with the kindest and most free-spirited heart. She was always smiling, and it could light the entire room up. Looking back on my childhood and my adult life, I never even remember Mom arguing or stressing. She was just a loving mother and best friend.

We love and miss you, Mom! We will not ever stop fighting, for justice, for you!

NC DEPARTMENT OF
**HEALTH AND
HUMAN SERVICES**
Division of Health Service Regulation

ROY COOPER · Governor

MANDY COHEN, MD, MPH · Secretary

MARK PAYNE · Director

September 4, 2018

Ms. Wanda Young
14 Morning Drive
Jacksonville, NC 28546

Dear Ms. Young:

You contacted the Complaint Intake Unit with concerns about the care residents received at Premier Nursing And Rehabilitation Center in Jacksonville. The Nursing Home Licensure and Certification Section of the Division of Health Service Regulation investigates your complaint in accordance with the Code of Federal Regulations, Title 42, §488.332 and North Carolina General Statute §131E-124.

A team of investigators inspected Premier Nursing And Rehabilitation Center in Jacksonville on July 29, 2018 to August 3, 2018. The team carefully investigated your specific concerns. Surveyors observed resident care, reviewed records and interviewed residents, staff and others, as needed. We did not substantiate the allegations. A substantiated finding means that noncompliance did occur and is verified by evidence. This could be based on the resident(s) you named, other residents, situations you described or similar situations. A substantiated finding could result in federal deficiencies, state deficiencies or no deficiencies. The reason a substantiated finding could result in no deficiencies is because at the time of the investigation, the nursing home had already taken action to correct the problem. An unsubstantiated finding means that there is a lack of evidence to support that noncompliance existed. This determination is not intended to minimize your concerns. To the contrary, we believe findings of this type provide feedback to the nursing home regarding the quality of care and services received by its residents.

See the attached Quick Report for a summary of the deficiencies found at the nursing home. The deficiencies may not be about the person for whom you filed the complaint. Every complainant receives the deficiency statement because it is a public record.

Your specific complaint investigation details are stored in a federal database and the Nursing Home Section is not authorised to release them. In order to receive the details of your specific complaint investigation, you must submit a letter to the Centers for Medicare and Medicaid Services, Bobby Cobb, Freedom of Information Group, 61 Forsyth Street SW Suite 4T20, Atlanta, GA 30303. Sample request letters can be found at https://www.cms.gov/Regulations-and-Guidance/Legislation/FOIA/filehow.html. Reference the intake number at the bottom of this letter and indicate $0 for the fee. If you do not have computer access, call this office and ask for a manager to assist you.

DIVISION OF HEALTH SERVICE REGULATION · NURSING HOME LICENSURE AND CERTIFICATION SECTION

LOCATION: 1205 UMSTEAD DRIVE · LINEBERGER BUILDING · RALEIGH, NC 27603
MAILING ADDRESS: 2711 MAIL SERVICE CENTER · RALEIGH, NC 27699-2711
www.ncdhhs.gov/dhsr ·TEL: 919-855-4520 · FAX 919-715-3290

AN EQUAL OPPORTUNITY / AFFIRMATIVE ACTION EMPLOYER

Ms. Young
September 4, 2018
Page 2

We hope that the complaint investigation details help you understand how we arrived at our complaint results, however, if you need to discuss the results, call a manager at the Nursing Home Section. The Nursing Home Licensure and Certification telephone number is 919-855-4520.

Thank you for sharing your concerns about the nursing home.

Sincerely,

Miranda Nixon
Facility Survey Consultant

MN: tc

Investigation Number: GNHA11
Intake Number: NC00141491

Attachments:
Quick Report

<table>
<tr><td colspan="2">DEPARTMENT OF HEALTH AND HUMAN SERVICES
CENTERS FOR MEDICARE & MEDICAID SERVICES</td><td>Quick Report Entire Survey</td></tr>
<tr><td>(X1) PROVIDER/SUPPLIER/CLIA
IDENTIFICATION NUMBER:

345217</td><td>NAME OF PROVIDER OR SUPPLIER, STREET ADDRESS, CITY, STATE, ZIP CODE
PREMIER NURSING AND REHABILITATION CENTER
225 WHITE STREET
JACKSONVILLE, NC 28546</td><td>(X3) DATE SURVEY
COMPLETED

08/03/2018</td></tr>
</table>

F 580
SS=D

Notify of Changes (Injury/Decline/Room, etc.)

§483.10(g)(14) Notification of Changes.
(i) A facility must immediately inform the resident; consult with the resident's physician; and notify, consistent with his or her authority, the resident representative(s) when there is-
(A) An accident involving the resident which results in injury and has the potential for requiring physician intervention;
(B) A significant change in the resident's physical, mental, or psychosocial status (that is, a deterioration in health, mental, or psychosocial status in either life-threatening conditions or clinical complications);
(C) A need to alter treatment significantly (that is, a need to discontinue an existing form of treatment due to adverse consequences, or to commence a new form of treatment); or
(D) A decision to transfer or discharge the resident from the facility as specified in §483.15(c)(1)(ii).
(ii) When making notification under paragraph (g)(14)(i) of this section, the facility must ensure that all pertinent information specified in §483.15(c)(2) is available and provided upon request to the physician.
(iii) The facility must also promptly notify the resident and the resident representative, if any, when there is-
(A) A change in room or roommate assignment as specified in §483.10(e)(6); or
(B) A change in resident rights under Federal or State law or regulations as specified in paragraph (e)(10) of this section.
(iv) The facility must record and periodically update the address (mailing and email) and phone number of the resident representative(s).

§483.10(g)(15)
Admission to a composite distinct part. A facility that is a composite distinct part (as defined in §483.5) must disclose in its admission agreement its physical configuration, including the various locations that comprise the composite distinct part, and must specify the policies that apply to room changes between its different locations under §483.15(c)(9).
Based on record reviews, family interview and staff interviews, the facility failed to notify the physician of Resident # 37 slipping of a Mechanical lift (sit to stand) and causing the straps to slip around the resident's neck which caused the resident's face to turn purplish blue in color. This was evident in 1 of 5 residents reviewed for accidents. (Resident # 37)

The findings included:

Resident # 37 was admitted on 11/12/2014 with diagnoses of Alzheimer's disease, cerebrovascular disease, dementia, generalized muscle weakness, pain and abnormal posture. The quarterly Minimum Data Set (MDS), dated 5/23/2018, indicated Resident # 37's cognition had been severely impaired and she had required extensive assistance of one person for bed mobility. Resident #37 had been totally dependent with the assistance of 2 staff for transfers, dressing and toileting. The MDS indicated Resident #37 was not steady when moving from a seated position to a standing position and had only able to stabilize with staff assistance.

Resident # 37's care plan, dated 3/18/2018, indicated Resident # 37 required "assistance for mobility due to the aging process, short and long term memory deficits, physical limitations/non-ambulatory, weakness, unsteady balance during transitions." The interventions included the following: monitor for safety awareness, transfers using mechanical lift (sit to stand lift) with aid of 2 persons, report to nurse any decrease in ability to transfer safely and monitor for safety awareness.

A review of Resident #37's Care Guide, updated 3/18/2018, and indicated the following: the resident required Activity of Daily Living (ADL) care, may require 2 person assist with toileting. Transfers: mechanical lift (sit to stand lift; vest size - L) with 2 person assist. The resident required non-skid footwear.

A review of a nurse's note, dated 6/23/2018, indicated Resident # 37 exhibited difficulty standing with a sit-to-stand lift per staff interview; 3 staff members assisted Resident # 37 onto the toilet when feet slipped off mechanical lift.

A review of the facility's incident log for Resident # 37 revealed no incident report had been completed after the 6/23/2018 incident.

During an interview with Resident #37's Responsible Party (RP) on 7/31/2018 at 2:00 PM, the RP reported on 6/23/2018 he came to visit Resident #37 and found her almost "choked" on the mechanical lift's straps. The RP indicated another nursing assistant (NA), NA #3, had been asked to come to Resident #37's room and assisted in getting her safely down to the bathroom floor or toilet seat. The RP reported he had been concerned about Resident #37's safety while being transferred on a mechanical lift. He further indicated the staff did not follow the guidelines as required while using the mechanical lift because he had noticed on the day of the accident she had been transferred by one nurse aide instead of two. The RP further reported Resident #37 had not been wearing shoes or nonskid socks per the care guide and the strap around the lower legs had not been applied.

During an interview with NA #1 on 8/1/2018 at 10:00 AM, NA # 1 reported she had been assigned to work with Resident # 37 on 6/23/2018. She indicated before lunch, she had been transferring the resident from the bed to the toilet with the sit-to-stand (mechanical lift) by herself. NA #1 reported Resident #37 started to slip from the lift before getting on the toilet. NA# 1 stated a family member had arrived for a visit and found Resident#37 had slipped from the mechanical lift. NA #1 stated the RP had started to assist to keep her from falling but had been unable to stop the resident from slipping and the strap from getting caught at the resident's neck. NA # 1 stated she left Resident # 37 on the lift in the bathroom to get more help from another staff member who had been in another resident's room at the end of the hall. NA #1 stated Medication Aide (MA) # 1 also came by the resident's bathroom but stood by the resident's room waiting for additional assistance to get the resident off the mechanical lift. NA #1 stated prior to the incident she had been in a panic to get Resident # 37 to the bathroom before the family's visit. She further added the family of Resident #37 had wanted Resident # 37 up in the mornings and she had no other person to ask for assistance. NA #1 added the day the resident had the accident the facility had been short of staff and she could not find anyone to

DEPARTMENT OF HEALTH AND HUMAN SERVICES CENTERS FOR MEDICARE & MEDICAID SERVICES		Quick Report Entire Survey
X1) PROVIDER/SUPPLIER/CLIA IDENTIFICATION NUMBER: 345217	NAME OF PROVIDER OR SUPPLIER, STREET ADDRESS, CITY, STATE, ZIP CODE **PREMIER NURSING AND REHABILITATION CENTER** **225 WHITE STREET** **JACKSONVILLE, NC 28546**	(X3) DATE SURVEY COMPLETED 08/03/2018

F 580   Continued From page 1

assist her with transferring Resident # 37 on the mechanical lift. NA #1 stated Resident #37 is always "dancing" (unsteady while standing) while being transferred on the mechanical lift, making it a more difficult transfer.

During an interview with NA #2 on 8/1/2018 at 10:20 AM, NA # 2 stated he came down to Resident # 37's room after he finished giving care to another patient. He had been told he needed to help Resident # 37 who had been left dangling from the mechanical lift. NA #2 indicated once he had arrived at Resident # 37's bathroom, he had noticed the resident's face was purplish blue and the lift's straps were by the resident's neck. NA # 2 reported he did not recall whether Resident # 37's knees were touching the floor or not because everything had happened so fast. He further indicated the resident head was tilted towards the front of her body. NA # 2 stated after he had assisted the resident to a seated position on the toilet the resident's color in her face returned to normal. NA # 2 stated the resident's family member had been in the room but had not assisted with getting the resident off the mechanical lift. NA #2 added NA # 1 assisted him with getting Resident # 37 off the lift. He indicated Nurse # 1 assessed Resident # 37 after the resident had been removed from the mechanical lift and had been placed on the toilet.

During an interview with MA #1 on 8/1/2018 at 10: 30 AM, MA # 1 stated NA # 1 had come out of Resident # 37's room and stated she needed help. MA #1 stated she had entered Resident # 37's room and she noticed the resident had been on the lift and had slipped down with her feet off the platform of the lift. MA # 1 indicated she had been waiting for NA # 1 to get more help as the patient had been constantly slipping. MA #1 added the resident's face had turned red in color as she slid down the lift. MA # 1 indicated the strap had slipped by the resident's neck.

During an interview with Nurse #1 on 8/1/2018 at 11:10 AM, Nurse # 1 stated she had been assigned to care for Resident #37 on 6/23/2018. Nurse #1 stated NA # 1 reported to her they had difficulty during the transfer of Resident #37 from the bed to the toilet using the mechanical lift. Nurse #1 stated Resident # 37 had slid off the lift because the staff failed to use the leg straps and nonskid socks or shoes which caused the resident to slip some from the lift. Nurse #1 reported NA # 1 had been using the lift with no assistance. She further stated she had expected the NA # 1 to have asked for assistance when using the lift. She indicated the lift required 2 persons. Nurse # 1 stated the use of nonskid socks or shoes had always been required to prevent residents' feet from slipping off the lift but they had not been used by NA # 1. Nurse #1 stated she had also felt the sit to stand lift was not appropriate for Resident # 37. Nurse # 1 indicated she had assessed Resident #37 after she had been transferred to the toilet by the NA's and stated she did not notice any injury to Resident #37. Nurse # 1 indicated she did not report the incident to the physician or the Director of Nursing (DON) because she did not think of Resident # 37's slip on the mechanical lift as an incident or accident. Nurse #1 stated in looking back at what had happened to the resident, she should have reported the incident to the physician, DON and completed an incident report.

During an interview with the Physician on 8/1/2018 at 11:30 AM, the Physician indicated he had not been made aware of Resident #37's incident on 6/23/2018. The physician indicated his expectation would have been for the facility staff to have notified him of the incident emphasizing especially if the resident had turned purple blue in color during the incident.

During the interview with the Staff Development Coordinator (SDC) on 8/2/2018 at 11:30 AM, the SDC stated NA # 2 reported to her, during the 08/01/2018 investigation of the incident involving Resident #37, when he had been asked to assist with Resident # 37 on 6/23/2018, she had seen the resident's face turned purple blue and the resident's veins bulged on her neck while she dangled on the mechanical lift. The SDC indicated she had thought a supervisor had investigated the incident after it happened on 6/23/2018 as she had overheard a conversation about the incident around the time it happened. She added she could not recall the exact date or the name of the supervisor. The SDC stated she had not been the SDC at the time of Resident # 37's mechanical lift accident.

During an interview with the DON on 8/2/2018 at 12:30 PM, the DON reported she had not been aware of Resident #37's incident of 6/23/2018 when the resident had slipped off the lift. The DON indicated her expectation of nursing staff would have been to have completed an incident report so she could have started an in-service training on the proper use of a mechanical lift. She further indicated her expectation was for the Physician to have been notified about the accident.

During an interview with the Administrator on 8/2/2018 at 12:40 PM, the Administrator reported he had just learned about the incident of Resident #37's slip off the mechanical lift. The Administrator stated his expectation would have been for the staff to have reported the accident to the DON immediately so they could have begun an in-service on the proper use of the mechanical lift. Administrator also reported his expectation was for the Physician to have been notified about the accident.

F 600
SS=J   Free from Abuse and Neglect

§483.12 Freedom from Abuse, Neglect, and Exploitation
The resident has the right to be free from abuse, neglect, misappropriation of resident property, and exploitation as defined in this subpart. This includes but is not limited to freedom from corporal punishment, involuntary seclusion and any physical or chemical restraint not required to treat the resident's medical symptoms.

§483.12(a) The facility must-

§483.12(a)(1) Not use verbal, mental, sexual, or physical abuse, corporal punishment, or involuntary seclusion;
Based on record reviews, observations, family interview and staff interviews, the facility neglected to follow manufacturer's guidelines by failing to attach and tighten the leg straps of the facility's mechanical lift around the resident's lower legs and failed to implement care plan

DEPARTMENT OF HEALTH AND HUMAN SERVICES
CENTERS FOR MEDICARE & MEDICAID SERVICES

Quick Report Entire Survey

(X1) PROVIDER/SUPPLIER/CLIA IDENTIFICATION NUMBER:	NAME OF PROVIDER OR SUPPLIER, STREET ADDRESS, CITY, STATE, ZIP CODE	(X3) DATE SURVEY COMPLETED
345217	**PREMIER NURSING AND REHABILITATION CENTER** **225 WHITE STREET** **JACKSONVILLE, NC 28546**	08/03/2018

F 600   Continued From page 2

and care guide interventions indicating use of 2 person assistance while transferring with the use of mechanical lift(sit to stand) and failed to ensure the resident had on non-skid footwear for 1 of 5 sampled residents reviewed for accidents. Resident #37 slipped during a transfer from the mechanical lift which allowed the lift's straps to slip around the resident ' s neck which caused the resident's face to turn purplish blue in color. Resident #37 was assessed at the facility and found to have no physical injuries.

Immediate Jeopardy for Resident # 37 began on 6/23/2018 when the resident slipped while only one staff member was transferring her using a mechanical lift and staff failed to properly secure her to the lift and ensure she was wearing non-skid foot and the lift's straps slipped around the resident's neck causing the resident's face to turn purplish blue. Immediate Jeopardy was remove on 8/2/2018 when the facility provided an acceptable credible allegation of Immediate Jeopardy removal. The facility will remain out of compliance at a scope and severity of D (not actual harm with potential for more than minimal harm that is not Immediate Jeopardy) to allow for ongoing in- servicing or monitoring to be accomplished.

The findings included:

A review of the manufacturer's manual instructions for the mechanical lift used at the facility, dated April 2013, included the following instructions: "Position the mechanical lift and adjust the width of the base, so that the patient's feet can be centered on the footrest. The lower legs (below the knees) should be parallel to the lower-leg on the lift. Adjust the horizontal and vertical position of the pad for comfortable resistance just below the kneecaps. Attach and tighten the strap around the lower legs."

Resident # 37 was admitted on 11/12/2014 with diagnoses of Alzheimer ' s disease, cerebrovascular disease, dementia, generalized muscle weakness, pain and abnormal posture.

The quarterly Minimum Data Set (MDS), dated 5/23/2018, indicated Resident # 37' s cognition had been severely impaired and she had required extensive assistance of one person for bed mobility. Resident #37 was totally dependent with the assistance of 2 staff for transfers, dressing and toileting. The MDS indicated Resident #37 was not steady when moving from a seated position to a standing position and was only able to stabilize with staff assistance. The MDS indicated Resident #37 was not steady when moving on and off the toilet and had only been able to stabilize with staff assistance. The MDS indicated Resident #37 had no trial of a toileting program and she had been frequently incontinent of her bowels and bladder.

Resident # 37's care plan, dated 5/23/2018 indicated Resident # 37 required "assistance for mobility due to the aging process, short and long term memory deficits, physical limitations/non-ambulatory, weakness, unsteady balance during transitions." The interventions included the following: monitor for safety awareness, transfers using mechanical lift (sit to stand lift) with aid of 2 persons, report to nurse any decrease in ability to transfer safely and monitor for safety awareness

A review of Resident #37's current Care Guide dated 5/23/2018 indicated the following: the resident required Activity of Daily Living (ADL) care, may require 2 person assist with toileting. Transfers: mechanical lift (sit to stand lift; vest size - L) with 2 person assist. The resident required non-skid footwear.

A review of a nurse's note, dated 6/23/2018 and written by Nurse # 1, indicated Resident # 37 exhibited difficulty standing with a sit-to-stand lift per staff interview; 3 staff members assisted Resident # 37 onto the toilet when her feet slipped off mechanical lift.
A review of the facility's incident log for Resident # 37 revealed no incident report had been completed after the 6/23/2018 incident.

During an interview with Resident #37's Responsible Party (RP) on 7/31/2018 at 2:00 PM, the RP reported on 6/23/2018 he came to visit Resident #37 and found her almost "choked" on the mechanical lift ' s straps. The RP indicated another nursing assistant (NA), NA #3, had been asked to come to Resident #37's room and assisted in getting her safely down to the bathroom floor or toilet seat. The RP reported he had been concerned about Resident #37's safety while being transferred on a mechanical lift. He further indicated the staff did not follow the guidelines as required while using the mechanical lift because he had noticed on the day of the accident she had been transferred by one nurse aide instead of two. The RP further reported Resident #37 had not been wearing shoes or nonskid socks per the care guide and the strap around the lower legs had not been applied.

During an interview with NA #1 on 8/1/2018 at 10:00 AM, NA # 1 reported she had been assigned to work with Resident # 37 on 6/23/2018. She indicated before lunch, she had been transferring the resident from the bed to the toilet with the sit-to-stand (mechanical lift) by herself. NA #1 reported Resident #37 started to slip from the lift before getting on the toilet. NA# 1 stated a family member had arrived for a visit and found Resident #37 had slipped from the mechanical lift. NA #1 stated the RP had started to assist to keep her from falling but had been unable to stop the resident from slipping and the strap from getting caught at the resident ' s neck. NA # 1 stated she left Resident # 37 on the lift in the bathroom to get more help from another staff member who had been in another resident ' s room at the end of the hall. NA #1 stated Medication Aide (MA) # 1 also came by the resident ' s bathroom but stood by the resident ' s room waiting for additional assistance to get the resident off the mechanical lift. NA #1 stated prior to the incident she had been in a panic to get Resident # 37 to the bathroom before the family ' s visit. She further added the family of Resident #37 had wanted Resident # 37 up in the mornings and she had no other person to ask for assistance. NA #1 added the day the resident had the accident the facility had been short of staff and she could not find anyone to assist her with transferring Resident # 37 on the mechanical lift. NA #1 stated Resident #37 is always "dancing" (unsteady while standing) while being transferred on the mechanical lift, making it a more difficult transfer.

During an interview with NA #2 on 8/1/2018 at 10:20 AM, NA # 2 stated he came down to Resident # 37's room after he finished giving

<table>
<tr><td colspan="2">DEPARTMENT OF HEALTH AND HUMAN SERVICES
CENTERS FOR MEDICARE & MEDICAID SERVICES</td><td>Quick Report Entire Survey</td></tr>
<tr><td>X1) PROVIDER/SUPPLIER/CLIA
IDENTIFICATION NUMBER:

345217</td><td>NAME OF PROVIDER OR SUPPLIER, STREET ADDRESS, CITY, STATE, ZIP CODE
PREMIER NURSING AND REHABILITATION CENTER
225 WHITE STREET
JACKSONVILLE, NC 28546</td><td>(X3) DATE SURVEY
COMPLETED

08/03/2018</td></tr>
</table>

F 600   Continued From page 3

care to another patient. He had been told he needed to help Resident # 37 who had been left dangling from the mechanical lift. NA #2 indicated once he had arrived at Resident # 37's bathroom, he had noticed the resident's face was purplish blue and the lift's straps were by the resident's neck. NA # 2 reported he did not recall whether Resident # 37's knees were touching the floor or not because everything had happened so fast. He further indicated the resident head was tilted towards the front of her body. NA # 2 stated after he had assisted the resident to a seated position on the toilet the resident's color in her face returned to normal. NA # 2 stated the resident's family member had been in the room but had not assisted with getting the resident off the mechanical lift. NA #2 added NA # 1 assisted him with getting Resident # 37 off the lift. He indicated Nurse # 1 assessed Resident # 37 after the resident had been removed from the mechanical lift and had been placed on the toilet.

During an interview with MA #1 on 8/1/2018 at 10: 30 AM, MA # 1 stated NA # 1 had come out of Resident # 37's room and stated she needed help. MA #1 stated she had entered Resident # 37's room and she noticed the resident had been on the lift and had slipped down with her feet off the platform of the lift. MA # 1 indicated she had been waiting for NA # 1 to get more help as the patient had been constantly slipping. MA #1 added the resident's face had turned red in color as she slid down the lift. MA # 1 indicated the strap had slipped by the resident's neck.

During an interview with Nurse #1 on 8/1/2018 at 11:10 AM, Nurse # 1 stated she had been assigned to care for Resident #37 on 6/23/2018. Nurse #1 stated NA # 1 reported to her they had difficulty during the transfer of Resident #37 from the bed to the toilet using the mechanical lift. Nurse #1 stated Resident # 37 had slid off the lift because the staff failed to use the leg straps and nonskid socks or shoes which caused the resident to slip some from the lift. Nurse #1 reported NA # 1 had been using the lift with no assistance. She further stated she had expected the NA # 1 to have asked for assistance when using the lift. She indicated the lift required 2 persons. Nurse # 1 stated the use of nonskid socks or shoes had always been required to prevent residents' feet from slipping off the lift but they had not been used by NA # 1. Nurse #1 stated she had also felt the sit to stand lift was not appropriate for Resident # 37. Nurse # 1 indicated she had assessed Resident #37 after she had been transferred to the toilet by the NA's and stated she did not notice any injury to Resident #37. Nurse # 1 indicated she did not report the incident to the physician or the Director of Nursing (DON) because she did not think of Resident # 37's slip on the mechanical lift as an incident or accident. Nurse #1 stated in looking back at what had happened to the resident, she should have reported the incident to the physician, DON and completed an incident report.

During an interview with the Physician on 8/1/2018 at 11:30 AM, the Physician indicated he had not been made aware of Resident #37's incident on 6/23/2018. The physician indicated his expectation would have been for the facility staff to have notified him of the incident emphasizing especially if the resident had turned purple blue during the incident.

During an interview with the MDS nurse on 8/2/2018 at 9:30 AM, the MDS nurse reported Resident #37 had history of being unstable while being transferred on a sit to stand lift because her legs had been buckling (both of knees give out). The MDS nurse stated the family had insisted on the use of the sit to stand lift even though the staff at the facility had been aware it had not been appropriate for Resident # 37.

During an observation of a mechanical lift transfer made on 8/2/2018 at 10:30 AM, Resident # 37's appeared confused with the instructions given her by NA # 4 to grasp the mechanical lift's sling bar. Resident # 37 had been noticed to be unsteady while standing on the lift.

During an interview with NA #4 on 8/2/2018 at 10:40 AM, NA# 4 reported Resident #37 had been unstable while on the lift but she had been transferred using the sit to stand lift for a long time. NA #4 indicated Resident # 37 had usually been assisted to the toilet before breakfast and lunch.

During the interview with the Staff Development Coordinator (SDC) on 8/2/2018 at 11:30 AM, the SDC stated NA # 2 reported to her, during the 08/01/2018 investigation of the incident involving Resident #37, when he had been asked to assist with Resident # 37 on 6/23/2018, she had seen the resident's face turned purple blue and the resident's veins bulged on her neck while she dangled on the mechanical lift. The SDC indicated she had thought a supervisor had investigated the incident after it happened on 6/23/2018 as she had overheard a conversation about the incident around the time it happened. She added she could not recall the exact date or the name of the supervisor. The SDC stated she had not been the SDC at the time of Resident # 37's mechanical's lift accident.

During an interview with the DON on 8/2/2018 at 12:30 PM, the DON reported she had not been aware of Resident #37's incident of 6/23/2018 when the resident had slipped off the lift. The DON indicated her expectation of nursing staff would have been to have completed an incident report so she could have started an in-service training on the proper use of a mechanical lift.

During an interview with the Administrator on 8/2/2018 at 12:40 PM, the Administrator reported he had just learned about the incident of Resident #37's slip off the mechanical lift. The Administrator stated his expectation would have been for the staff to have reported the accident to the DON immediately so they could have begun an in-service on the proper use of the mechanical lift.

The Administrator, Director of Nursing and Facility's nurse consultant were notified of the Immediate Jeopardy on 8/1/2018 at 4:30 pm.

On 8/2/2018 the facility provided an acceptable credible allegation for immediate jeopardy removal that included the following:

Corrective Actions
On 8/1/18, interviews were initiated by the Social Workers with all alert and oriented residents.
The resident concern process will be followed by the social worker and Administrator for all identified areas of concern by 8/2/18.

<table>
<tr><td colspan="2">DEPARTMENT OF HEALTH AND HUMAN SERVICES
CENTERS FOR MEDICARE & MEDICAID SERVICES</td><td>Quick Report Entire Survey</td></tr>
<tr><td>(X1) PROVIDER/SUPPLIER/CLIA
IDENTIFICATION NUMBER:

345217</td><td>NAME OF PROVIDER OR SUPPLIER, STREET ADDRESS, CITY, STATE, ZIP CODE
PREMIER NURSING AND REHABILITATION CENTER
225 WHITE STREET
JACKSONVILLE, NC 28546</td><td>(X3) DATE SURVEY
COMPLETED

08/03/2018</td></tr>
</table>

F 600   Continued From page 4

On 8/1/18, a transfer observation of 100% of all residents to include resident # 37 utilizing mechanical lifts was initiated by the Minimum Data Set (MDS) coordinator, MDS nurses and therapy manager. The purpose of the observation is to ensure that the resident's current mechanical lift use is the safest method of transfer. The audit will be completed by 8/2/18. The MDS coordinator will re-evaluate the resident transfer method, update the resident care plan and care guide, and complete a therapy referral by 8/2/18 for any identified areas of safety concerns observed during the audit.

On 8/1/18, a questionnaire was initiated with 100% of all nurses and nursing assistants by the Quality Improvement (QI) nurse. This questionnaire will be completed by 8/2/18. The MDS coordinator will re-evaluate the resident transfer method, update the resident care plan and care guide, and complete a therapy referral by 8/2/18 for any identified areas of safety concerns expressed during the questionnaire. After 8/2/18, all nurses and nursing assistants that have not completed the questionnaire will not be allowed to work until the questionnaire is completed.

On 8/1/18, return demonstrations of mechanical lift transfer was initiated with 100% of all nurses and nursing assistants by the Staff Facilitator. The purpose of the return demonstrations are to ensure that staff are checking the resident care guide for the correct number of person to utilize for transfers and that the mechanical lift is being utilized per manufacture specifications during the transfer. After, 8/2/18, all nurses and nursing assistants that have not completed the return demonstration will not be allowed to work until the return demonstration is completed.

On 8/1/18 an audit of all resident's incident reports to include resident # 37 from 6/23/18 to 8/1/18 was initiated by the MDS nurses and the treatment nurse to ensure all incidents have been thoroughly investigated to determine the root cause and appropriate interventions initiated to prevent further incidents. This audit will be completed by 8/2/18. The QI nurse will investigate the incident, implement interventions, and update the resident care plan and care guide by 8/2/18 for all identified areas of concern.

On 8/1/18 an audit of all resident's progress notes to include resident # 37 from 6/23/18 to 8/1/18 was initiated by the QI nurse and the Registered Nurse (RN) supervisor to ensure that all documented incidents have an incident report, was investigated to determine the root cause and appropriate interventions were implemented to prevent further incidents. This audit will be completed by 8/2/18. The QI nurse will investigate the incident, implement interventions, and update the resident care plan and care guide by 8/2/18 for all identified areas of concern.

On 8/01/18, an in-service was initiated for 100% of all staff to include nurses, nursing assistants, housekeeping, dietary, therapy, maintenance, pay roll, book keeper, social workers, was initiated by the Staff Facilitator regarding Neglect to include examples of neglect and prevention of neglect. This in-service was completed by 8/02/18. After 8/2/18, all staff to include nurses, nursing assistants, housekeeping, dietary, therapy, maintenance, pay roll, book keeper, social workers that have not worked and/or not received the in-services will be mailed the in-service via certified mail by the Payroll Bookkeeper. Instructions will be included in the in-service packet to read, sign the in-service, call the Staff Facilitator or Director of Nursing with any questions, and return the signed in-service to the Staff Facilitator or Director of Nursing prior to next schedule shift. Staff will not be permitted to work until the signed in services are received.

On 8/1/18 an in-service was initiated by the Staff Facilitator with 100% of all nurses and nursing assistants regarding the safe handling and movement policy. This in-service included reading the resident care guide to identify the number of person required for resident transfer, reporting to the nurse when a transfer method is no longer safe, lowering the resident and not leaving the resident when sliding in the lift and how to safely strap and transfer resident in the mechanical lift per the manufacture specifications. The manufacture specification will be printed by the Staff Facilitator and reviewed with staff during the in-service. This in-service will be completed by 8/2/18. After 8/2/18, all nurses and nursing assistants that have not worked and/or not received the in-services will be mailed via certified mail by the Payroll Bookkeeper. Instructions will be included in the in-service packet to read, sign the in-service, call the Staff Facilitator or Director of Nursing with any questions, and return the signed in-service to the Staff Facilitator or Director of Nursing prior to next schedule shift. Staff will not be permitted to work until the signed in services are received.

The Administrator, Director of Nursing, and Quality Improvement nurse was in serviced on the process of investigating incidents on 8/1/18 by the Facility Nurse Consultant. The in-service included to review the incident reports 5 days per week, how to pull a report from the risk management portal in the electronic records to identify incidents that have been documented by the nurses, printing the incident reports from the electronic records, flagging the incident for follow up, reading progress notes to identify all incidents, discussing incidents in the clinical morning meetings, determining the root cause of the incident, completion of incident reports, and implementing and monitoring interventions.

An in-service was completed with the Director of Nursing on 8/2/18 regarding requirements for re-evaluating residents for change in transfer methods by the Facility Nurse Consultant.

On 8/1/18 an in-service was initiated by the Staff Facilitator with 100% of all nurses regarding completion of incident reports and collecting witness statements. After 8/2/18, all nurses that has not worked and/or not received the in-service will be mailed the in-service via certified mail by the Payroll Bookkeeper. Instructions will be included in the in-service packet to read, sign the in-service, call the Staff Facilitator or Director of Nursing with any questions, and return the signed in-service to the Staff Facilitator or Director of Nursing prior to next schedule shift. Staff will not be permitted to work until the signed in services are received.

The decision to monitor the system for prevention of accidents was made on 8/1/2018 by the Administrator and Director of Nursing. The RN Supervisor, the Staff Facilitator, Treatment nurse, Unit Facilitator and/or the QI nurses, will audit 10% of all residents requiring

<table>
<tr><td colspan="2">DEPARTMENT OF HEALTH AND HUMAN SERVICES
CENTERS FOR MEDICARE & MEDICAID SERVICES</td><td>Quick Report Entire Survey</td></tr>
<tr><td>(X1) PROVIDER/SUPPLIER/CLIA
IDENTIFICATION NUMBER:

345217</td><td>NAME OF PROVIDER OR SUPPLIER, STREET ADDRESS, CITY, STATE, ZIP CODE
PREMIER NURSING AND REHABILITATION CENTER
225 WHITE STREET
JACKSONVILLE, NC 28546</td><td>(X3) DATE SURVEY
COMPLETED

08/03/2018</td></tr>
</table>

F 600   Continued From page 5

mechanical lifts for transfers to include resident # 37 to ensure staff are checking the resident care guide and utilizing the number of person identified on the care guide, staff are utilizing the mechanical lift per manufacture specification during the transfer, and ensure the current lift is the safest method of transfer 3 x a week for four weeks, then weekly for x 4 weeks, then monthly x 1 month utilizing a Lift Transfer Audit Tool. Any areas of concern will be immediately addressed by the RN Supervisor, the Staff Facilitator, the Unit Facilitator and/or the QI nurses to include staff retraining. The Director of Nursing will review and initial the Lift Transfer Audit Tools weekly x 8 weeks then monthly x 1 month.

The Registered Nurse (RN) Supervisor, the Staff Facilitator, Treatment nurse, Unit Facilitator and/or the QI nurses will review all incidents reports and progress notes 3 x a week for 4 weeks, then weekly for x 4 weeks, then monthly x 1 month utilizing the Incident Audit Tool to ensure all identified incidents have been thoroughly investigated, incidents reports completed, and appropriate interventions implemented to prevent further accidents. The RN Supervisor, the Staff Facilitator, Treatment nurse, Unit Facilitator and/or the QI nurses will investigate the incident, implement interventions, and provide retraining for all identified areas of concern during the audit. The Director of Nursing will review and initial the Incident Audit Tool weekly x 8 weeks then monthly x 1 month.

The Quality Improvement Organization will be contacted by the Director of Nursing on 8/02/18 for assistance in evaluation of specific steps to be taken to address neglect and prevention of accidents and training, staff position/title designated to be responsible for the steps, timeline for accomplishment of the steps, specific methodology to be used to evaluate the plan ' s success, and frequency of monitoring the effects of the plan initiation.

The DON will present the findings of the Lift Transfer Audit Tools and the Incident Audit Tools to the Executive Quality Assurance (QA) committee monthly for 3 months. The Executive QA Committee will meet monthly for 3 months and review the Lift Transfer Audit Tools and the Incident Audit Tools to determine trends and/or issues that may need further interventions put into place and to determine the need for further frequency of monitoring. The decision to review the monitoring of prevention of accidents during the quality assurance committee meeting was made by the Administrator and Director of Nursing on 8/01/2018.

Final date of compliance is 8/02/2018.

The Administrator and DON will be responsible for the implementation of corrective actions to include all 100% audits, in services, and monitoring related to the plan of correction.

The Credible Allegation for Immediate Jeopardy removal was validated on 8/2/2018, which removed the Immediate Jeopardy on 8/2/2018. During the Immediate Jeopardy removal validation process interviews were conducted with nursing staff present in the facility on 8/2/2018. The staff confirmed the recent in- services and training of the proper use of Mechanical lift. Reviews of the in-service records, audit tools, audits performed and facility assessments were made. Observations of residents' transfers were completed.

F 656
SS=D   Develop/Implement Comprehensive Care Plan

§483.21(b) Comprehensive Care Plans
§483.21(b)(1) The facility must develop and implement a comprehensive person-centered care plan for each resident, consistent with the resident rights set forth at §483.10(c)(2) and §483 10(c)(3), that includes measurable objectives and timeframes to meet a resident's medical, nursing, and mental and psychosocial needs that are identified in the comprehensive assessment. The comprehensive care plan must describe the following -
(i) The services that are to be furnished to attain or maintain the resident's highest practicable physical, mental, and psychosocial well-being as required under §483.24, §483.25 or §483.40; and
(ii) Any services that would otherwise be required under §483.24, §483.25 or §483.40 but are not provided due to the resident's exercise of rights under §483.10, including the right to refuse treatment under §483.10(c)(6).
(iii) Any specialized services or specialized rehabilitative services the nursing facility will provide as a result of PASARR recommendations. If a facility disagrees with the findings of the PASARR, it must indicate its rationale in the resident's medical record.
(iv)In consultation with the resident and the resident's representative(s)-
(A) The resident's goals for admission and desired outcomes.
(B) The resident's preference and potential for future discharge. Facilities must document whether the resident's desire to return to the community was assessed and any referrals to local contact agencies and/or other appropriate entities, for this purpose.
(C) Discharge plans in the comprehensive care plan, as appropriate, in accordance with the requirements set forth in paragraph (c) of this section.
Based on record reviews, family interview and staff interviews, the facility failed to implement care plan and care guide interventions indicating use of 2 person assistance while transferring with the use of mechanical lift (sit to stand) and the use of nonskid footwear for 1 of 5 sampled residents (Resident # 37)

The findings Included:

Resident # 37 was admitted on 11/12/2014 with diagnoses of Alzheimer's disease, cerebrovascular disease, dementia, generalized muscle weakness, pain and abnormal posture. The quarterly Minimum Data Set (MDS), dated 5/23/2018, indicated Resident # 37's cognition had been severely impaired and she had required extensive assistance of one person for bed mobility. Resident #37 had been totally dependent with the assistance of 2 staff for transfers, dressing and toileting. The MDS indicated Resident #37 was not steady when moving from a

DEPARTMENT OF HEALTH AND HUMAN SERVICES
CENTERS FOR MEDICARE & MEDICAID SERVICES

Quick Report Entire Survey

(X1) PROVIDER/SUPPLIER/CLIA IDENTIFICATION NUMBER:	NAME OF PROVIDER OR SUPPLIER, STREET ADDRESS, CITY, STATE, ZIP CODE	(X3) DATE SURVEY COMPLETED
345217	**PREMIER NURSING AND REHABILITATION CENTER** **225 WHITE STREET** **JACKSONVILLE, NC 28546**	08/03/2018

F 656   Continued From page 6

seated position to a standing position and had only able to stabilize with staff assistance. The MDS indicated Resident #37 was not steady when moving on and off the toilet and had only been able to stabilize with staff assistance

Resident # 37's care plan, dated 3/18/2018, indicated Resident # 37 required "assistance for mobility due to the aging process, short and long term memory deficits, physical limitations/non-ambulatory, weakness, unsteady balance during transitions." The interventions included the following: monitor for safety awareness, transfers using mechanical lift (sit to stand lift) with aid of 2 persons, report to nurse any decrease in ability to transfer safely and monitor for safety awareness.

A review of Resident #37's Care Guide, updated 3/18/2018, and indicated the following: the resident required Activity of Daily Living (ADL) care, may require 2 person assist with toileting. Transfers: mechanical lift (sit to stand lift; vest size - L) with 2 person assist. The resident required non-skid footwear.

A review of a nurse's note, dated 6/23/2018, indicated Resident # 37 exhibited difficulty standing with a sit-to-stand lift per staff interview; 3 staff members assisted Resident # 37 onto the toilet when feet slipped off mechanical lift.

During an interview with Resident #37's Responsible Party (RP) on 7/31/2018 at 2:00 PM, the RP reported on 6/23/2018 he came to visit Resident #37 and found her almost "choked" on the mechanical lift's straps. The RP indicated another nursing assistant (NA), NA #3, had been asked to come to Resident #37's room and assisted in getting her safely down to the bathroom floor or toilet seat. The RP reported he had been concerned about Resident #37's safety while being transferred on a mechanical lift. He further indicated the staff did not follow the guidelines as required while using the mechanical lift because he had noticed on the day of the accident she had been transferred by one nurse aide instead of two. The RP further reported Resident #37 had not been wearing shoes or nonskid socks per the care guide and the strap around the lower legs had not been applied.

During an interview with NA #1 on 8/1/2018 at 10:00 AM, NA # 1 reported she had been assigned to work with Resident # 37 on 6/23/2018. She indicated before lunch, she had been transferring the resident from the bed to the toilet with the sit-to-stand (mechanical lift) by herself. NA #1 reported Resident #37 started to slip from the lift before getting on the toilet. NA# 1 stated a family member had arrived for a visit and found Resident #37 had slipped from the mechanical lift. NA #1 stated the RP had started to assist to keep her from falling but had been unable to stop the resident from slipping and the strap from getting caught at the resident's neck. NA # 1 stated she left Resident # 37 on the lift in the bathroom to get more help from another staff member who had been in another resident's room at the end of the hall. NA #1 stated

Medication Aide (MA) # 1 also came by the resident's bathroom but stood by the resident's room waiting for additional assistance to get the resident off the mechanical lift. NA #1 stated prior to the incident she had been in a panic to get Resident # 37 to the bathroom before the family's visit. She further added the family of Resident #37 had wanted Resident # 37 up in the mornings and she had no other person to ask for assistance. NA #1 added the day the resident had the accident the facility had been short of staff and she could not find anyone to assist her with transferring Resident # 37 on the mechanical lift. NA #1 stated Resident #37 is always "dancing" (unsteady while standing) while being transferred on the mechanical lift, making it a more difficult transfer.

During an interview with NA #2 on 8/1/2018 at 10:20 AM, NA # 2 stated he came down to Resident # 37's room after he finished giving care to another patient. He had been told he needed to help Resident # 37 who had been left dangling from the mechanical lift. NA #2 indicated once he had arrived at Resident # 37's bathroom, he had noticed the resident's face was purplish blue and the lift's straps were by the resident's neck. NA # 2 reported he did not recall whether Resident # 37's knees were touching the floor or not because everything had happened so fast. He further indicated the resident head was tilted towards the front of her body. NA # 2 stated after he had assisted the resident to a seated position on the toilet the resident's color in her face returned to normal. NA # 2 stated the resident's family member had been in the room but had not assisted with getting the resident off the mechanical lift. NA #2 added NA # 1 assisted him with getting Resident # 37 off the lift. He indicated Nurse # 1 assessed Resident # 37 after the resident had been removed from the mechanical lift and had been placed on the toilet.

During an interview with Nurse #1 on 8/1/2018 at 11:10 AM, Nurse # 1 stated she had been assigned to care for Resident #37 on 6/23/2018. Nurse #1 stated NA # 1 reported to her they had difficulty during the transfer of Resident #37 from the bed to the toilet using the mechanical lift. Nurse #1 stated Resident # 37 had slid off the lift because the staff failed to use the leg straps and nonskid socks or shoes which caused the resident to slip some from the lift. Nurse #1 reported NA # 1 had been using the lift with no assistance. She further stated she had expected the NA # 1 to have asked for assistance when using the lift. She indicated the lift required 2 persons. Nurse # 1 stated the use of nonskid socks or shoes had always been required to prevent residents' feet from slipping off the lift but they had not been used by NA # 1. Nurse #1 stated she had also felt the sit to stand lift was not appropriate for Resident # 37. Nurse # 1 indicated she had assessed Resident #37 after she had been transferred to the toilet by the NA's and stated she did not notice any injury to Resident #37. Nurse # 1 indicated she did not report the incident to the physician or the Director of Nursing (DON) because she did not think of Resident # 37's slip on the mechanical lift as an incident or accident. Nurse #1 stated in looking back at what had happened to the resident, she should have reported the incident to the physician, DON and completed an incident report.

During an interview with the DON on 8/2/2018 at 12:30 PM, the DON reported she had not been aware of Resident #37's incident of 6/23/2018 when the resident had slipped off the lift. The DON indicated her expectation of nursing staff would have been to have completed an incident report so she could have started an in-service training on the proper use of a mechanical lift. She also stated her expectation was for the staff to follow the care plan.

031799

<table>
<tr><td colspan="2">DEPARTMENT OF HEALTH AND HUMAN SERVICES
CENTERS FOR MEDICARE & MEDICAID SERVICES</td><td>Quick Report Entire Survey</td></tr>
<tr><td>(X1) PROVIDER/SUPPLIER/CLIA
IDENTIFICATION NUMBER:

345217</td><td>NAME OF PROVIDER OR SUPPLIER, STREET ADDRESS, CITY, STATE, ZIP CODE

PREMIER NURSING AND REHABILITATION CENTER
225 WHITE STREET
JACKSONVILLE, NC 28546</td><td>(X3) DATE SURVEY
COMPLETED

08/03/2018</td></tr>
</table>

F 656   Continued From page 7

During an interview with the Administrator on 8/2/2018 at 12:40 PM, the Administrator reported he had just learned about the incident of Resident #37's slip off the mechanical lift. The Administrator stated his expectation would have been for the staff to have reported the accident to the DON immediately so they could have begun an in-service on the proper use of the mechanical lift. He indicated his expectation was for the staff to follow the care plan.

F 689
SS=J   Free of Accident Hazards/Supervision/Devices

§483.25(d) Accidents.
The facility must ensure that -
§483.25(d)(1) The resident environment remains as free of accident hazards as is possible; and

§483.25(d)(2)Each resident receives adequate supervision and assistance devices to prevent accidents.
Based on record reviews, observations, family interview, physician interview and staff interviews, the facility failed to attach and tighten the mechanical lift's leg straps around the lower legs per manufacturer's guidelines and failed to implement care plan and care guide interventions indicating use of 2 person assistance while transferring with the use of mechanical lift (sit to stand) and failed to ensure the resident had on non-skid footwear for 1 of 5 sampled residents reviewed for accidents. Resident #37 slipped during a transfer from the mechanical lift which allowed the lift's straps to slip around the resident's neck which caused the resident's face to turn purplish blue in color. Resident #37 was assessed at the facility and found to have no physical injuries.

Immediate Jeopardy for Resident # 37 began on 6/23/2018 when the resident slipped while only one staff member was transferring her using a mechanical lift and staff failed to properly secure her to the lift and ensure she was wearing non-skid foot and the lift's straps slipped around the resident's neck causing the resident's face to turn purplish blue. Immediate Jeopardy was remove on 8/2/2018 when the facility provided an acceptable credible allegation of Immediate Jeopardy removal. The facility will remain out of compliance at a scope and severity of D (not actual harm with potential for more than minimal harm that is not Immediate Jeopardy) to allow for ongoing in- servicing or monitoring to be accomplished.

The findings included:

A review of the manufacturer's manual instructions for the mechanical lift used at the facility, dated April 2013, included the following instructions: "Position the mechanical lift and adjust the width of the base, so that the patient's feet can be centered on the footrest. The lower legs (below the knees) should be parallel to the lower-leg on the lift. Adjust the horizontal and vertical position of the pad for comfortable resistance just below the kneecaps. Attach and tighten the strap around the lower legs."

Resident # 37 was admitted on 11/12/2014 with diagnoses of Alzheimer's disease, cerebrovascular disease, dementia, generalized muscle weakness, pain and abnormal posture.

The quarterly Minimum Data Set (MDS), dated 5/23/2018, indicated Resident # 37's cognition had been severely impaired and she had required extensive assistance of one person for bed mobility. Resident #37 had been totally dependent with the assistance of 2 staff for transfers, dressing and toileting. The MDS indicated Resident #37 was not steady when moving from a seated position to a standing position and was only able to stabilize with staff assistance. The MDS indicated Resident #37 was not steady when moving on and off the toilet and had only been able to stabilize with staff assistance. The MDS indicated Resident #37 had no trial of a toileting program and she had been frequently incontinent of her bowels and bladder.

Resident # 37's care plan, dated 5/23/2018 indicated Resident # 37 required "assistance for mobility due to the aging process, short and long term memory deficits, physical limitations/non-ambulatory, weakness, unsteady balance during transitions." The interventions included the following: monitor for safety awareness, transfers using mechanical lift (sit to stand lift) with aid of 2 persons, report to nurse any decrease in ability to transfer safely and monitor for safety awareness

A review of Resident #37's current Care Guide dated 5/23/2018 indicated the following: the resident required Activity of Daily Living (ADL) care, may require 2 person assist with toileting. Transfers: mechanical lift (sit to stand lift; vest size - L) with 2 person assist. The resident required non-skid footwear.

A review of a nurse's note, dated 6/23/2018 and written by Nurse # 1, indicated Resident # 37 exhibited difficulty standing with a sit-to-stand lift per staff interview; 3 staff members assisted Resident # 37 onto the toilet when her feet slipped off mechanical lift.

A review of the facility's incident log for Resident # 37 revealed no incident report had been completed after the 6/23/2018 incident.

During an interview with Resident #37's Responsible Party (RP) on 7/31/2018 at 2:00 PM, the RP reported on 6/23/2018 he came to visit Resident #37 and found her almost "choked" on the mechanical lift's straps. The RP indicated another nursing assistant (NA), NA #3, had been asked to come to Resident #37's room and assisted in getting her safely down to the bathroom floor or toilet seat. The RP reported he had been concerned about Resident #37's safety while being transferred on a mechanical lift. He further indicated the staff did not follow the guidelines as required while using the mechanical lift because he had noticed on the day of the accident she had been transferred by one nurse aide instead of two. The RP further reported Resident #37 had not been wearing shoes or nonskid socks per the care guide and the strap around the lower legs had not been applied.

<table>
<tr><td colspan="2">DEPARTMENT OF HEALTH AND HUMAN SERVICES
CENTERS FOR MEDICARE & MEDICAID SERVICES</td><td>Quick Report Entire Survey</td></tr>
<tr><td>(X1) PROVIDER/SUPPLIER/CLIA
IDENTIFICATION NUMBER:

345217</td><td>NAME OF PROVIDER OR SUPPLIER, STREET ADDRESS, CITY, STATE, ZIP CODE
PREMIER NURSING AND REHABILITATION CENTER
225 WHITE STREET
JACKSONVILLE, NC 28546</td><td>(X3) DATE SURVEY
COMPLETED

08/03/2018</td></tr>
</table>

F 689   Continued From page 8

During an interview with NA #1 on 8/1/2018 at 10:00 AM, NA # 1 reported she had been assigned to work with Resident # 37 on 6/23/2018. She indicated before lunch, she had been transferring the resident from the bed to the toilet with the sit-to-stand (mechanical lift) by herself. NA #1 reported Resident #37 started to slip from the lift before getting on the toilet. NA# 1 stated a family member had arrived for a visit and found Resident #37 had slipped from the mechanical lift. NA #1 stated the RP had started to assist to keep her from falling but had been unable to stop the resident from slipping and the strap from getting caught at the resident's neck. NA # 1 stated she left Resident # 37 on the lift in the bathroom to get more help from another staff member who had been in another resident's room at the end of the hall. NA #1 stated Medication Aide (MA) # 1 also came by the resident's bathroom but stood by the resident's room waiting for additional assistance to get the resident off the mechanical lift. NA #1 stated prior to the incident she had been in a panic to get Resident # 37 to the bathroom before the family's visit. She further added the family of Resident #37 had wanted Resident # 37 up in the mornings and she had no other person to ask for assistance. NA #1 added the day the resident had the accident the facility had been short of staff and she could not find anyone to assist her with transferring Resident # 37 on the mechanical lift. NA #1 stated Resident #37 is always "dancing" (unsteady while standing) while being transferred on the mechanical lift, making it a more difficult transfer.

During an interview with NA #2 on 8/1/2018 at 10:20 AM, NA # 2 stated he came down to Resident # 37's room after he finished giving care to another patient. He had been told he needed to help Resident # 37 who had been left dangling from the mechanical lift. NA #2 indicated once he had arrived at Resident # 37's bathroom, he had noticed the resident's face was purplish blue and the lift's straps were by the resident's neck. NA # 2 reported he did not recall whether Resident # 37's knees were touching the floor or not because everything had happened so fast. He further indicated the resident head was tilted towards the front of her body. NA # 2 stated after he had assisted the resident to a seated position on the toilet the resident's color in her face returned to normal. NA # 2 stated the resident's family member had been in the room but had not assisted with getting the resident off the mechanical lift. NA #2 added NA# 1 assisted him with getting Resident # 37 off the lift. He indicated Nurse # 1 assessed Resident # 37 after the resident had been removed from the mechanical lift and had been placed on the toilet.

During an interview with MA #1 on 8/1/2018 at 10:30 AM, MA # 1 stated NA # 1 had come out of Resident # 37's room and stated she needed help. MA# 1 stated she had entered Resident # 37's room and she noticed the resident had been on the lift and had slipped down with her feet off the platform of the lift. MA # 1 indicated she had been waiting for NA # 1 to get more help as the patient had been constantly slipping. MA #1 added the resident's face had turned red in color as she slid down the lift. MA # 1 indicated the strap had slipped by the resident's neck.

During an interview with Nurse #1 on 8/1/2018 at 11:10 AM, Nurse # 1 stated she had been assigned to care for Resident #37 on 6/23/2018. Nurse #1 stated NA # 1 reported to her they had difficulty during the transfer of Resident #37 from the bed to the toilet using the mechanical lift. Nurse #1 stated Resident # 37 had slid off the lift because the staff failed to use the leg straps and nonskid socks or shoes which caused the resident to slip some from the lift. Nurse #1 reported NA # 1 had been using the lift with no assistance. She further stated she had expected the NA # 1 to have asked for assistance when using the lift. She indicated the lift required 2 persons. Nurse # 1 stated the use of nonskid socks or shoes had always been required to prevent residents' feet from slipping off the lift but they had not been used by NA # 1. Nurse #1 stated she had also felt the sit to stand lift was not appropriate for Resident # 37. Nurse # 1 indicated she had assessed Resident #37 after she had been transferred to the toilet by the NA's and stated she did not notice any injury to Resident #37. Nurse # 1 indicated she did not report the incident to the physician or the Director of Nursing (DON) because she did not think of Resident # 37's slip on the mechanical lift as an incident or accident. Nurse #1 stated in looking back at what had happened to the resident, she should have reported the incident to the physician, DON and completed an incident report.

During an interview with the Physician on 8/1/2018 at 11:30 AM, the Physician indicated he had not been made aware of Resident #37's incident on 6/23/2018. The physician indicated his expectation would have been for the facility staff to have notified him of the incident emphasizing especially if the resident had turned purple blue during the incident.

During an interview with the MDS nurse on 8/2/2018 at 9:30 AM, the MDS nurse reported Resident #37 had history of being unstable while being transferred on a sit to stand lift because her legs had been buckling (both of knees give out). The MDS nurse stated the family had insisted on the use of the sit to stand lift even though the staff at the facility had been aware it had not been appropriate for Resident # 37.

During an observation of a mechanical lift transfer made on 8/2/2018 at 10:30 AM, Resident # 37's appeared confused with the instructions given her by NA # 4 to grasp the mechanical lift's sling bar. Resident # 37 had been noticed to be unsteady while standing on the lift.

During an interview with NA #4 on 8/2/2018 at 10:40 AM, NA# 4 reported Resident #37 had been unstable while on the lift but she had been transferred using the sit to stand lift for a long time. NA #4 indicated Resident # 37 had usually been assisted to the toilet before breakfast and lunch.

During the interview with the Staff Development Coordinator (SDC) on 8/2/2018 at 11:30 AM, the SDC stated NA # 2 reported to her, during the 08/01/2018 investigation of the incident involving Resident #37, when he had been asked to assist with Resident # 37 on 6/23/2018, she had seen the resident's face turned purple blue and the resident's veins bulged on her neck while she dangled on the mechanical lift. The SDC indicated she had thought a supervisor had investigated the incident after it happened on 6/23/2018 as she had overheard a conversation about the incident around the time it happened. She added she could not recall the exact date or the name of the supervisor. The SDC stated she had not been the SDC at the time of Resident # 37's mechanical's lift accident.

During an interview with the DON on 8/2/2018 at 12:30 PM, the DON reported she had not been aware of Resident #37's incident of

<table>
<tr><td colspan="2">DEPARTMENT OF HEALTH AND HUMAN SERVICES
CENTERS FOR MEDICARE & MEDICAID SERVICES</td><td>Quick Report Entire Survey</td></tr>
<tr><td>(X1) PROVIDER/SUPPLIER/CLIA
IDENTIFICATION NUMBER:

345217</td><td>NAME OF PROVIDER OR SUPPLIER, STREET ADDRESS, CITY, STATE, ZIP CODE
PREMIER NURSING AND REHABILITATION CENTER
225 WHITE STREET
JACKSONVILLE, NC 28546</td><td>(X3) DATE SURVEY
COMPLETED

08/03/2018</td></tr>
</table>

F 689 Continued From page 9

6/23/2018 when the resident had slipped off the lift. The DON indicated her expectation of nursing staff would have been to have completed an incident report so she could have started an in-service training on the proper use of a mechanical lift.

During an interview with the Administrator on 8/2/2018 at 12:40 PM, the Administrator reported he had just learned about the incident of Resident #37's slip off the mechanical lift. The Administrator stated his expectation would have been for the staff to have reported the accident to the DON immediately so they could have begun an in-service on the proper use of the mechanical lift.

The Administrator, Director of Nursing and Facility's nurse consultant were notified of the Immediate Jeopardy on 8/1/2018 at 4:30 pm.

On 8/2/2018 the facility provided an acceptable credible allegation for immediate jeopardy removal that included the following:

Corrective Actions:

On 8/01/18, interviews were initiated by the Social Workers with all alert and oriented residents.
The resident concern process will be followed by the social worker and Administrator for all identified areas of concern by 8/2/18.

On 8/1/18, a transfer observation of 100% of all residents to include resident # 37 utilizing mechanical lifts was initiated by the Minimum Data Set (MDS) coordinator, MDS nurses and therapy manager. The purpose of the observation is to ensure that the resident's current mechanical lift use is the safest method of transfer. The audit will be completed by 8/2/18. The MDS coordinator will re-evaluate the resident transfer method, update the resident care plan and care guide, and complete a therapy referral by 8/2/18 for any identified areas of safety concerns observed during the audit.

On 8/1/18, a questionnaire was initiated with 100% of all nurses and nursing assistants by the Quality Improvement (QI) nurse. This questionnaire will be completed by 8/2/18. The MDS coordinator will re-evaluate the resident transfer method, update the resident care plan and care guide, and complete a therapy referral by 8/2/18 for any identified areas of safety concerns expressed during the questionnaire. After 8/2/18, all nurses and nursing assistants that have not completed the questionnaire will not be allowed to work until the questionnaire is completed.

On 8/1/18, return demonstrations of mechanical lift transfer was initiated with 100% of all nurses and nursing assistants by the Staff Facilitator. The purpose of the return demonstrations are to ensure that staff are checking the resident care guide for the correct number of person to utilize for transfers and that the mechanical lift is being utilized per manufacture specifications during the transfer. After, 8/2/18, all nurses and nursing assistants that have not completed the return demonstration will not be allowed to work until the return demonstration is completed.

On 8/1/18 an audit of all resident's incident reports to include resident # 37 from 6/23/18 to 8/1/18 was initiated by the MDS nurses and the treatment nurse to ensure all incidents have been thoroughly investigated to determine the root cause and appropriate interventions initiated to prevent further incidents. This audit will be completed by 8/2/18. The QI nurse will investigate the incident, implement interventions, and update the resident care plan and care guide by 8/2/18 for all identified areas of concern.

On 8/1/18 an audit of all resident's progress notes to include resident # 37 from 6/23/18 to 8/1/18 was initiated by the QI nurse and the Registered Nurse (RN) supervisor to ensure that all documented incidents have an incident report, was investigated to determine the root cause and appropriate interventions were implemented to prevent further incidents. This audit will be completed by 8/2/18. The QI nurse will investigate the incident, implement interventions, and update the resident care plan and care guide by 8/2/18 for all identified areas of concern.

On 8/01/18, an in-service was initiated for 100% of all staff to include nurses, nursing assistants, housekeeping, dietary, therapy, maintenance, pay roll, book keeper, social workers, was initiated by the Staff Facilitator regarding Neglect to include examples of neglect and prevention of neglect. This in-service was completed by 8/02/18. After 8/2/18, all staff to include nurses, nursing assistants, housekeeping, dietary, therapy, maintenance, pay roll, book keeper, social workers that have not worked and/or not received the in-services will be mailed the in-service via certified mail by the Payroll Bookkeeper. Instructions will be included in the in-service packet to read, sign the in-service, call the Staff Facilitator or Director of Nursing with any questions, and return the signed in-service to the Staff Facilitator or Director of Nursing prior to next schedule shift. Staff will not be permitted to work until the signed in services are received.
On 8/1/18 an in-service was initiated by the Staff Facilitator with 100% of all nurses and nursing assistants regarding the safe handling and movement policy. This in-service included reading the resident care guide to identify the number of person required for resident transfer, reporting to the nurse when a transfer method is no longer safe, lowering the resident and not leaving the resident when sliding in the lift and how to safely strap and transfer resident in the mechanical lift per the manufacture specifications. The manufacture specification will be printed by the Staff Facilitator and reviewed with staff during the in-service. This in-service will be completed by 8/2/18. After 8/2/18, all nurses and nursing assistants that have not worked and/or not received the in-services will be mailed via certified mail by the Payroll Bookkeeper. Instructions will be included in the in-service packet to read, sign the in-service, call the Staff Facilitator or Director of Nursing with any questions, and return the signed in-service to the Staff Facilitator or Director of Nursing prior to next schedule shift. Staff will not be permitted to work until the signed in services are received.

The Administrator, Director of Nursing, and Quality Improvement nurse was in serviced on the process of investigating incidents on 8/1/18 by the Facility Nurse Consultant. The in-service included to review the incident reports 5 days per week, how to pull a report from the risk management portal in the electronic records to identify incidents that have been documented by the nurses, printing the incident reports from

DEPARTMENT OF HEALTH AND HUMAN SERVICES
CENTERS FOR MEDICARE & MEDICAID SERVICES

Quick Report Entire Survey

(X1) PROVIDER/SUPPLIER/CLIA IDENTIFICATION NUMBER:	NAME OF PROVIDER OR SUPPLIER, STREET ADDRESS, CITY, STATE, ZIP CODE	(X3) DATE SURVEY COMPLETED
345217	**PREMIER NURSING AND REHABILITATION CENTER** **225 WHITE STREET** **JACKSONVILLE, NC 28546**	08/03/2018

F 689　Continued From page 10

the electronic records, flagging the incident for follow up, reading progress notes to identify all incidents, discussing incidents in the clinical morning meetings, determining the root cause of the incident, completion of incident reports, and implementing and monitoring interventions.

An in-service was completed with the Director of Nursing on 8/2/18 regarding requirements for re -evaluating residents for change in transfer methods by the Facility Nurse Consultant.

On 8/1/18 an in-service was initiated by the Staff Facilitator with 100% of all nurses regarding completion of incident reports and collecting witness statements. After 8/2/18, all nurses that has not worked and/or not received the in-service will be mailed the in-service via certified mail by the Payroll Bookkeeper. Instructions will be included in the in-service packet to read, sign the in-service, call the Staff Facilitator or Director of Nursing with any questions, and return the signed in-service to the Staff Facilitator or Director of Nursing prior to next schedule shift. Staff will not be permitted to work until the signed in services are received.

The decision to monitor the system for prevention of accidents was made on 8/1/2018 by the Administrator and Director of Nursing. The RN Supervisor, the Staff Facilitator, Treatment nurse, Unit Facilitator and/or the QI nurses, will audit 10% of all residents requiring mechanical lifts for transfers to include resident # 37 to ensure staff are checking the resident care guide and utilizing the number of person identified on the care guide, staff are utilizing the mechanical lift per manufacture specification during the transfer, and ensure the current lift is the safest method of transfer 3 x a week for four weeks, then weekly for x 4 weeks, then monthly x 1 month utilizing a Lift Transfer Audit Tool. Any areas of concern will be immediately addressed by the RN Supervisor, the Staff Facilitator, the Unit Facilitator and/or the QI nurses to include staff retraining. The Director of Nursing will review and initial the Lift Transfer Audit Tools weekly x 8 weeks then monthly x 1 month.

The Registered Nurse (RN) Supervisor, the Staff Facilitator, Treatment nurse, Unit Facilitator and/or the QI nurses will review all incidents reports and progress notes 3 x a week for 4 weeks, then weekly for x 4 weeks, then monthly x 1 month utilizing the Incident Audit Tool to ensure all identified incidents have been thoroughly investigated, incidents reports completed, and appropriate interventions implemented to prevent further accidents. The RN Supervisor, the Staff Facilitator, Treatment nurse, Unit Facilitator and/or the QI nurses will investigate the incident, implement interventions, and provide retraining for all identified areas of concern during the audit. The Director of Nursing will review and initial the Incident Audit Tool weekly x 8 weeks then monthly x 1 month.

The Quality Improvement Organization will be contacted by the Director of Nursing on 8/02/18 for assistance in evaluation of specific steps to be taken to address neglect and prevention of accidents and training, staff position/title designated to be responsible for the steps, timeline for accomplishment of the steps, specific methodology to be used to evaluate the plan ' s success, and frequency of monitoring the effects of the plan initiation.

The DON will present the findings of the Lift Transfer Audit Tools and the Incident Audit Tools to the Executive Quality Assurance (QA) committee monthly for 3 months. The Executive QA Committee will meet monthly for 3 months and review the Lift Transfer Audit Tools and the Incident Audit Tools to determine trends and/or issues that may need further interventions put into place and to determine the need for further frequency of monitoring. The decision to review the monitoring of prevention of accidents during the quality assurance committee meeting was made by the Administrator and Director of Nursing on 8/01/2018.

Final date of compliance is 8/02/2018.

The Administrator and DON will be responsible for the implementation of corrective actions to include all 100% audits, in services, and monitoring related to the plan of correction.

The Credible Allegation for Immediate Jeopardy removal was validated on 8/2/2018, which removed the Immediate Jeopardy on 8/2/2018. During the Immediate Jeopardy removal validation process interviews were conducted with nursing staff present in the facility on 8/2/2018. The staff confirmed the recent in- services and training of the proper use of Mechanical lift. Reviews of the in-service records, audit tools, audits performed and facility assessments were made. Observations of residents' transfers were completed.

F 761
SS=D　Label/Store Drugs and Biologicals

§483.45(g) Labeling of Drugs and Biologicals
Drugs and biologicals used in the facility must be labeled in accordance with currently accepted professional principles, and include the appropriate accessory and cautionary instructions, and the expiration date when applicable.

§483.45(h) Storage of Drugs and Biologicals

§483.45(h)(1) In accordance with State and Federal laws, the facility must store all drugs and biologicals in locked compartments under proper temperature controls, and permit only authorized personnel to have access to the keys.

§483.45(h)(2) The facility must provide separately locked, permanently affixed compartments for storage of controlled drugs listed in Schedule II of the Comprehensive Drug Abuse Prevention and Control Act of 1976 and other drugs subject to abuse, except when the facility uses single unit package drug distribution systems in which the quantity stored is minimal and a missing dose can be readily detected.

<table>
<tr><td colspan="2">DEPARTMENT OF HEALTH AND HUMAN SERVICES
CENTERS FOR MEDICARE & MEDICAID SERVICES</td><td>Quick Report Entire Survey</td></tr>
<tr><td>(X1) PROVIDER/SUPPLIER/CLIA
IDENTIFICATION NUMBER:

345217</td><td>NAME OF PROVIDER OR SUPPLIER, STREET ADDRESS, CITY, STATE, ZIP CODE

PREMIER NURSING AND REHABILITATION CENTER
225 WHITE STREET
JACKSONVILLE, NC 28546</td><td>(X3) DATE SURVEY
COMPLETED

08/03/2018</td></tr>
</table>

F 761   Continued From page 11

Based on observation and staff interview, the facility failed to dispose/discard expired medications in 1 of 3 medication storage rooms (Front Medication Room) and in 1 of 4 medication carts observed (300/400 Hall Medication Aide Cart).

The findings included:

During an observation of the medication refrigerator in the Front Medication Room on 07/30/18 at 5:10 p.m., the refrigerator contained 124 pre-filled syringes of Fluvirin (influenza vaccine) with an expiration date of May 2018.

During an observation of the nurse aide medication cart for the 300/400 hall on 08/02/18 at 11:30 a.m., a plastic storage bag was found to contain three expired bottles of medications:
Woman's Laxative expired February 2013, Gas Relief May 2018 and Omega XL expired July 2018.

During an interview with Nurse #1 on 07/30/18 at 5:15 p.m., Nurse #1 stated it was the responsibility of the hall nurses to keep the medication rooms free of expired medications.

During an interview with Medication Aide (MA) #1 on 08/02/18 at 11 30 a.m., MA #1 stated she did not know how the expired medication got into her medication cart.

During an interview with the Director of Nursing (DON) on 07/30/18 at 5:40 p.m., the DON stated it had been a joint effort of the nursing supervisors and the hall nurses to keep the medication rooms and medication carts free of expired medications. The DON stated it was her expectation nursing staff remove expired medication from the medication rooms and carts as soon as it is noticed.

About the Author

Heather T. Edgell lives in Jacksonville, North Carolina with her family. She has worked for the United State Marine Corps and the postal service, and she is currently in the process of opening an at-home health-care business to help other families experience peace of mind during long-term, palliative, and hospice care. She is married, has one adult child, and has four grandchildren, who are her pride and joy.

www.ingramcontent.com/pod-product-compliance
Lightning Source LLC
Chambersburg PA
CBHW051406150726
48000CB00003B/1356